SI UNITS
FOR NURSES

SI UNITS
FOR NURSES

J.A. Glenn
British Campus,
University of Evansville

and

D. McCaugherty
School of Nursing,
Princess Margaret Hospital,
Swindon

Harper & Row, Publishers

Cambridge
Hagerstown
Philadelphia
New York

San Francisco
Mexico City
Sao Paulo
Sydney

568677

First published 1981
Harper & Row
28 Tavistock Street
London WC2E 7PN

British Library Cataloguing in Publication Data

Glenn, John
  S. I. units for nurses.
  1. Nursing
  2. Metric system
  I. Title   II. McCaugherty, David
  530.8'12'024613

  ISBN 0-06-318180-0

QC
95
.G44
1981

Typeset by Colset Pte Ltd, Singapore
Printed and bound by The Blackmore Press, Dorset

CONTENTS

FOREWORD

This is not a book on SI units in general, but restricts itself to those measurements of clinical importance at the level of basic nursing care. The work of selecting relevant units has been done by the authors, and we hope that there is nothing in it that will not prove directly useful to entrants to the profession and their tutors. We are not writing for anyone else. Our thanks are due to students of the School of Nursing at Princess Margaret Hospital, Swindon, who helped in evaluating and checking the examples, and to Sheila Harris who typed the final text.

PREFACE FOR TUTORS

This book is written for all students of nursing taking basic training courses. It will also help those established nurses who still feel themselves unfamiliar with what is now standard hospital practice, who may still find SI a source of anxiety.

Although metric units have been used systematically and almost exclusively in schools and examinations since about 1970, it remains true that many entrants to nursing find difficulty in coping with normal hospital requirements in measure and calculation with measure. These entrants may include mature students with but hazy memories of school mathematics, or trainees from overseas who may not have had the advantage of being taught from a modern syllabus.

This book is an attempt to deal with that part of SI that applies to modern clinical practice, and does not concern itself with units not generally found in use in one department or another of a hospital. Although compiled for the student's use, we have not set out to provide a step-by-step 'programmed text'. Our aim is to help the reader to become familiar with the system, able to 'think metric' and aware that we now have a fully developed international system of units and symbols, adequate for all clinical and indeed all scientific or technical purposes of measurement. To give some background to this we include brief historical and expository notes, some discussion of normal ranges, incidental information on drug dosages, and so on. Our central theme, though, is the range of units and symbols that the nurse will need to understand and use.

1

This is not a book for armchair reading. We assume that the reader is involved in a course of training and that the normal measuring equipment of a hospital is available and in use. The book is to be referred to during training as necessary, and is not intended to be assimilated as a preliminary to training.

We also take it that some nurses will embark on postbasic or postregistration courses that demand rather more understanding of clinical or physiological measurement. Because of this, we have, especially in sections 5 and 6, gone a little way beyond the immediate daily needs of the newly trained nurse. A student could, on a first reading, be asked to work through sections 1, 2, 3, 4 and 7 only, but with the other sections available the text is a complete account of SI in the service of nursing care.

There will probably be two distinct groups of students or readers using this book. The first will be what we hope is the normal entry to the nursing profession, often with O levels including mathematics and a science subject calling for laboratory work. In any case they will be students reasonably familiar with the metric measures that have been used almost exclusively in schools for some years past.

The second group will be those who for some reason have missed out — and will probably recognize themselves as having missed out — on what should by now be basic instruction. They will be unfamiliar with SI units, even in their earlier metric forms, and may have little grasp of decimal calculations.

The first group will need to select from their general background those units and processes of importance to their chosen profession, to revise these and to become completely familiar with them in the special circumstances of nursing care. It is also to be hoped that understanding will go beyond the mere ability to use the units. We have tried to make this relevant selection from the complete system and to discuss it in a way that gives it professional substance.

For the second group (and any members of it who are reading this will certainly agree) the most effective help is personal tuition. If everyone could grasp a topic by working through a text book, teachers and tutors would have little to do except assess progress. This book, however, does contain the irreducible minimum of information required to provide for students, in the words of an adviser to the text, "clarification of the really essential measures so that they do not kill someone with an overdose". We hope that a reader in difficulty can, with tutorial advice, be guided through selected parts of this book at a first reading.

Nursing calls for a level of mathematical — or more plainly numerical — competence that is elementary but nevertheless indispensable. This is a work on SI, not a textbook of arithmetic, but to help matters at one of the notorious sticking points we include, as an appendix, a brief survey of decimal calculations, restricted to such numbers and processes as are likely to be needed in nursing practice. Its necessary compression assumes that the work has been done before at some time during the student's school days. If more is needed, only a course of class instruction or personal coaching can provide it satisfactorily.

We also include as an appendix a Diagnostic Test which can be given to students early in their careers. Those who do reasonably well on this can be asked to work quickly through the book to close up any gaps in their knowledge. Those who do not should work more slowly, perhaps under tutorial supervision, and in any event asking for guidance where it is needed.

The book is intended for self-instruction under guidance, but some tutors may wish to use it as a teaching text. It could be used as such in those schools or further education colleges that run prenursing courses for interested pupils. If any more information on number skills among entrants to professions is needed, tutors and teachers are referred to Glenn, J., *The Third R : Towards a Numerate Society* (Harper and Row 1978).

Note on Answers to Tests

The answers to all sectional and progress tests are given at the foot of the page opening following the test. It is more convenient for the reader to turn a page to see the results than to search through a list at the end of a book.

INTRODUCTION FOR READERS

This book is designed to introduce you to metric measures in the fully international system known as SI, and pays particular attention to those units that are now used in hospitals throughout the world. You will probably have met many of them before, both in school and, increasingly, in daily life; but a few of them, taken from science or technology because of their application to medicine, may be new to you. You will meet and have to deal with these during your training and career as a nurse, and in time they will become completely familiar.

You have a double problem. You must learn to handle SI and make measurements accurately using metricated apparatus. You must also learn to 'think metric', to judge litres and kilograms as easily as some older people can judge pints or pounds. It is always a great help in clinical measurement if you have some idea of what the result should be, and you will need to become used to the normal ranges of what you will be recording. Moreover, because you are now working with an international system, do learn to write the units and their symbols in their correct form. Copy carefully the symbols used in this book, and be on your guard against older and now obsolete forms used in many textbooks written before the present international agreement. Most important standard textbooks have been amended or corrected for their recent editions, but you are still working at the end of a transition period and you may find a few inconsistencies.

Work through the book at your own speed, and do all the exercises even if you think you know the subject matter. We are aiming at the familiarity that can only come with practice. This will, in the end, depend on the use you make of SI in your daily work, but the wide range of examples given should prepare you for whatever comes.

Any calculations you need to do will be with fractions and decimals. Only very simple processes are wanted for general use and you should be able to cope with them. If not, you can refer to Appendix 2 on decimal calculation. You could work through this first if you feel uncertain about using decimals. You will find that it deals only with the numbers and calculations you are likely to meet. If you cannot cope with the appendix, a more extended course of number work is needed, and you should consult a tutor.

Before beginning, read through the diagnostic test in Appendix 4. If you can do it, you are unlikely to have trouble in the use of SI measures, but in any case write down the answers and compare them with the key on p. 66. You should be able to do the entire test: any gaps will require filling by referring to the appropriate sections of the programme. If you have any difficulty with the test, read and work through the book with care.

When you have finished the sections, you should have a general understanding of SI. In particular you should be able to explain and use where necessary those SI units that are needed in hospitals.

Here is a preliminary list of the units of measurement we shall study:

1. The unit of length — the **metre**
2. The unit of mass — the **kilogram**
3. The unit of volume for liquids and gases — the **litre**
4. The unit of pressure — the **pascal**
5. The unit of energy — the **joule**
6. The unit of amount of substance — the **mole**
7. The unit of temperature — the **degree Celsius** (or Centigrade).

We shall also discuss the multiplying prefixes that turn the given units into larger or smaller units for convenience in measure and the correct way of writing quantities using the units and their symbols. You will then have learnt everything you will actually *need* about the units of measurement used in your profession. The skill in using them with accuracy and confidence cannot be learnt from a book. This is essential practical work, but the basic knowledge is not practical but theoretical. This knowledge the text that follows should help you to acquire.

THE BACKGROUND TO SI

Our former system of weights and measures, the old imperial units, was never planned, but developed over a long period of history. The original metric system, devised in France in 1795 at the time of the Revolution, was a deliberate attempt to construct a set of units for all scientific or technical purposes then known. It was at first based on a single unit of length but was modified as it developed.

The imperial measures spread widely in the wake of British colonialism, but the greater consistency of the French system led to its gradual adoption elsewhere. Its logical pattern allowed the metric system to produce new units when required for a developing technology, but in the end it was found that the old metric units were not standardized precisely enough for the needs of modern science. A series of international conferences discussed the problems of measurement in science and technology and eventually a revised and extended system of metric units, using most of the old names and relationships, was agreed in 1960. This is the Système International d'Unités — SI for short. It is now the accepted international language for measurement in science, industry and general use. In particular, it is illegal in the United Kingdom to prescribe or dispense drugs in any other units.

Anyone familiar with the old metric system will have no difficulty in adapting to SI. The advantages of the system are immense, even though the imperial measures had certain properties useful to particular local trades or interests. Every scientist, engineer, student or medical worker throughout the world can use the same language of units — quite literally with the same words and symbols, however their own language is written. Here, from a modern Japanese schoolbook, is a problem about a train 180 metres long travelling at 15 metres per second and crossing a bridge of length 210 metres.

長さ 180 m の電車が秒速 15 m で走るとき，長さ 210m の鉄橋をわたり終わるのに，何秒かかるでしょうか。

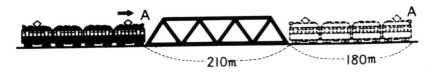

You may not be able to read the Japanese, but you can read the SI. It is not called Système International without good reason!

SI uses seven so-called *fundamental* units, but you will not need all of them. Fundamental units are those which are not made up of other units. These are defined with scientific precision and between them they meet every need of measurement from within atomic nuclei to large-scale engineering. There are many derived units to serve a wide range of use, but each derived unit is formed, as you will see, from two or more of the fundamental units.

In this book you will find a reference to 'basic' units. This is the word we have used to describe the units of measure needed in hospital, in their original form, before adding prefixes that make them larger or smaller. They are the ones that you, as a nurse, will need to know. Of the seven units on p. 5, nos. 1, 2, 6 and 7 are fundamental to SI, 3, 4, and 5 are derived using the fundamental measures; but they are all basic to hospital needs and can hardly be avoided by the nurse in training, on the level of understanding if not of everyday use. An easy example of a *derived* measure is that of speed, which relates the two fundamental measures of *length* (or distance) and *time*. Speed, however, is not a 'basic' measure for medical purposes.

BEGINNING SI

Early in your training you will meet the measuring instruments of your daily work as a nurse. Some, like scales, will be familiar, although they might be designed specially for hospital use. Others, like clinical thermometers and the indispensable sphygmomanometer, may be new to you. You will, inevitably, learn to use these in practice sessions, but confidence in interpreting their readings needs to be based on a firm knowledge of the units of measure used.

Do not try to work through this book at one or two sittings. Work through one section or less at a time as your other work calls for the units discussed. If the book has done its job, you should find it easy to complete the sectional tests, but by spreading the work out the daily repetition of words and symbols will most effectively impress itself on your memory and be reflected in your confidence. Please write down the answers to the tests and keep them; it is not enough to go through them orally.

Each section gives you the information you need to take you through one stage in the complete study. There may be introductory or additional paragraphs to make clear what is being done under the specific conditions of clinical practice. Any special instructions should be followed carefully. Remember that you are not merely engaged in an academic exercise. The difference between correct and incorrect measure and calculation may be a matter of life or death for the patients in your care. If you find yourself in any difficulties, consult your tutor; a word of explanation may be all you need.

LARGE AND SMALL: THE MULTIPLYING PREFIXES

The imperial measures used quite different units for large or small quantities. One weighed coal in tons and drugs in grains. SI does not do this; it uses a single unit and a standard set of multiplying prefixes which turn it into units of a convenient size, larger or smaller. The patient is weighed in kilograms, the drug in milligrams. The basic unit here is the same: the gram. The prefix kilo- gives us a measure one thousand times *bigger*, and the prefix milli- a measure one thousand times *smaller*.

SI has sixteen of these multiplying prefixes, which are used in exactly the same way for all measures, but only four are commonly found in hospital practice. You will soon learn these, as you work through the sections. Two of them have been given already in the last paragraph.

The complete list, for reference only, is given in Appendix 1. You may sometimes meet one or another of these in a textbook, and it is useful to have them.

A note on writing numbers

Note carefully how numbers are printed throughout this book. Large numbers used to express quantities are no longer, in modern printing, divided into groups of three digits by commas, but by spaces, working from the right, or from the left after a decimal point:

earlier printing	1,246,371
modern printing	1 246 371

The exception to this rule is a number having four digits only, which is printed without spacing or commas:

1000

9263

English speaking countries usually use a full stop on the line for a decimal point, although most countries use a comma both in print and writing. This is one reason why we no longer use the comma to space digits:

decimal point (English language)	1.96
decimal point (other countries)	1,96

If there are no digits in front of a decimal point, a zero must always be inserted

incorrect	.32
correct	0.32

This zero calls attention to the point and helps to keep the digits in the proper columns when numbers are being added.

In your own notes and written work follow the examples as given; but remember that you may meet obsolete usage in older textbooks. The spacing rules do not apply to code numbers, bank account references and the like.

For many years those who need to deal with very large or very small quantities have used a clever way of avoiding long and difficult to read strings of zeros in numbers, such as:

1 000 000 000

2 700 000

0.000 000 001

These are difficult to read and clumsy to write. In modern medical literature, when such numbers arise, it is now usual to adopt the mathematician's 'index notation'.

This uses a small raised number called the *index*, which in effect counts products of ten:

$$100 = 10 \times 10 = 10^2$$
$$1\ 000 = 10 \times 10 \times 10 = 10^3$$

$$10\,000 = 10 \times 10 \times 10 \times 10 = 10^4$$
and so on.

It follows that one million is 10^6, and this is easier to write than either the word or the string of six zeros required by the number 1 000 000. The notation easily extends to much larger numbers. A million million is 10^{12}, and a thousand million million is 10^{15}. Since five million is five times one million this number can be written as 5×10^6, six thousand million as 6×10^9, and so on.

For small numbers we use the index with a negative or minus sign: it represents the number of times we *divide* a unit by ten:

$$0.1 = 1/10$$
$$0.01 = 1/100$$
$$0.001 = 1/1000$$
and so on.

These fractions are written 10^{-1}, 10^{-2}, 10^{-3}, and so on, and this can be extended as before

$$0.000\,000\,1 = 1/1\,000\,000$$
$$= 10^{-6}$$

For normal hospital measurement of dosage and the like these large or small numbers are not used since it is the *unit* that is adjusted to be large or small by adding a prefix. They may, however, occur when *counting* is involved. Then this compact and easily read notation is most useful. As an example, one may see that the number of red corpuscles in a litre of blood is about 5×10^{12}. This expression is obviously more compact and less prone to errors in reading or writing than 5 000 000 000 000.

SECTION 1

MEASURING LENGTH: THE METRE

The metre is a fundamental unit of SI and is used to measure length and distance. It is a little longer than the old imperial yard. It was originally intended to be related to the circumference of the earth (it was to be one ten millionth of the distance from the Equator to the North Pole), but it is now given in terms of the wave length of light. If you have never used a metre rule, try to borrow one and measure, very roughly, the length and width of a room, the height of doors or windows, the length of tables and so on. Look at the metre rule and try to judge lengths and distances *before* you measure them. Pull out lengths of thread or mark off lengths with chalk which you judge to be about a metre, and check by measurement.

The prefixes kilo-, milli- and micro-

Your work with the metre rod makes it clear that it is not by itself a convenient unit for all purposes. It is a very small unit compared with a journey, a very large one compared with a bacterium. A patient in need of exercise might be told to walk a certain distance, stitches may need inserting at carefully judged intervals, or you may need to know the dimensions of bacteria or blood corpuscles. For such purposes the three prefixes most commonly used in hospitals are:

kilo-   giving kilometre, one thousand metres
milli- giving millimetre, one thousandth of a metre

micro- giving micrometre, one millionth of a metre

A kilometre is about a quarter of an hour's walk, the diameter of a 1p coin is 20 millimetres, the diameter of a red blood corpuscle is 7 or 8 micrometres. The micrometre is commonly used in textbooks discussing microscopic structures. In the older books it is often called the micron, written with the Greek letter μ, but this is now becoming obsolete. By using these prefixes you can express widely different sizes in manageable numbers. Such lengths are not usually written in full, but before beginning to use the symbols, write down the answers to these questions, which are given only for practice in reading the prefixes.

1. How many metres are there in one kilometre?
2. How many micrometres are there in one millimetre?
3. What part of a kilometre is a metre?
4. Express a kilometre in micrometres.
5. What part of a metre is a micrometre?
6. What fraction of a kilometre is a millimetre?
7. How many metres equal ten kilometres?
8. Express a millimetre in micrometres.
9. Express half a millimetre in micrometres.
10. How many metres are there in a kilometre and a half?

The answers are given at the foot of p. 14.
Note that in the USA metre is spelled *meter*, so that micrometre is spelled micrometer. In standard English spelling a micrometer is an accurate measuring instrument, not a unit.

Some more prefixes

There are three other prefixes which are occasionally used in hospital or clinical work. Two of them are common in the countries already using the metric system. These are:

deci-   giving decimetre, one tenth of a metre
centi-   giving centimetre, one hundredth of a metre

and, rarely found outside scientific papers,

nano-   giving nanometre, one thousand millionth of a metre.

It is better to think of a nanometre as one thousandth of a micrometre. Of these three, the centimetre is normally used for heights, important for height/weight ratios. The others are given for completeness. If you are unfamiliar with the units, use a centimetre/millimetre ruler to measure articles such as books or pencils. Try to estimate before you measure.

Write the answers to these questions (use numerals, not words):

1. How many decimetres are there in a kilometre?
2. Express one millimetre in nanometres.
3. Express one centimetre in millimetres.
4. How many centimetres are there in one decimetre?
5. Write one centimetre in micrometres.

The answers are at the foot of p. 16.

The use of the symbols

The international symbol for the metre is a lower case m, and the symbols for the prefixes we shall need are as follows:

kilo-   k
deci-   d

Answers from p. 13.
These are the answers, written in full for reference:

1. one thousand	6. one millionth
2. one thousand	7. ten thousand
3. one thousandth	8. one thousand micrometres
4. one thousand million	9. five hundred micrometres
5. one millionth	10. one thousand five hundred

Obviously such written numbers are clumsy and would not be used in either scientific or clinical texts, where the answers would probably appear as:

1. 1000	6. 10^{-6}
2. 1000	7. 10^4 or 10 000
3. 0.001	8. 1000 (micrometres)
4. 10^9	9. 500 (micrometres)
5. 10^{-6}	10. 1500

centi-	c
milli-	m
micro-	μ
nano-	n

Note that all these prefixes are lower case letters, not capitals. The symbols for micro is once again the Greek letter μ pronounced *mu*. It is, however, *read* as micro-.

Here is the total range of lengths written with the prefix symbols:

kilometre	km	1000 m
metre	m	1 m
decimetre*	dm	0.1 m
centimetre	cm	0.01 m
millimetre	mm	0.001 m or 10^{-3} m
micrometre	μm	0.000 001 m or 10^{-6} m
nanometre*	nm	0.000 000 001 m or 10^{-9} m

Of these, the two marked* are unlikely to be met in frequent use. It is very important on this international system to get the symbols *exactly* right. The unit symbols are symbols not abbreviations and they do not carry a full stop unless at the end of a sentence. Nor do they change their form for plurals: it is 10 cm NOT 10 cms. Such plural forms, which would not be recognized as such by speakers of most other languages, arose during the nineteenth century and are now obsolete. Here are some examples of the correct way to write units of length:

1. 10 km
2. 0.3 km
3. 192 cm
4. 15 mm
5. 1500 m

Now try to answer the following questions, writing all answers in numerical form with the correct symbols. In this and all following exercises write fractional quantities as decimals unless question requires otherwise.

Progress test 1

1. Write 10 km as metres.

2. Convert 100 μm to millimetres.
3. Express 15 cm as millimetres.
4. Express 15 mm as centimetres.
5. Write a height of 173 cm as metres.
6. Convert 2.36 mm to micrometres.
7. Write 1723 m as kilometres.
8. How many decimetres in 1.5 m?
9. Express 0.03 μm as nanometres.
10. Convert 5.2 km to metres.
11. Convert 5.2 mm to centimetres.
12. The dimensions of a file card are 15 cm × 5 cm. Express these in millimetres.
13. Express 1.3 dm as millimetres.
14. Write 0.021 mm as micrometres.
15. How many centimetres are equivalent to 235 mm?

The answers are at the foot of p. 18.

Answers from p. 14.
1. 10 000 or 10^4
2. 10^6 nanometres
3. 10 millimetres
4. 10
5. 10 000 or 10^4 micrometres

SECTION 2

MEASURING MASS: THE KILOGRAM

The SI fundamental unit of mass is the kilogram, one thousand grams. The kilogram, at the time of writing, is the mass of a cylinder of metal kept at Sèvres in France. It is commonly met as the mass (or weight) of a standard packet of sugar.

A healthy baby at birth normally weighs 3 – 4 kilograms.

Try to get used to guessing weights in grams and kilograms. Keep the packet of sugar in mind for the kilogram, and get into the habit of looking at the weights printed on packets of biscuits, tea and, of course, various hospital supplies. You will have to get used to weighing patients in kilograms. Always try to size them up and guess before you weigh. If you are used to stones and pounds and you have a weighing machine that gives both readings, try to look at the metric scale first and ignore the other: it is no longer of clinical importance, although patients will no doubt ask for their weight in stones and pounds. You can help them learn SI by emphasizing the kilograms.

Your own work will never call for practical measurement in other than kilograms or grams, but the milligram is the standard unit for most drugs and the microgram for some. You must be able to work with them.

In ordinary speech, we do not distinguish between the words 'mass' and 'weight'. For scientific purposes there is a clear distinction that is worth making, even though we shall not need to use it. The following note may be helpful:

The *mass* of a body can be measured by the force we have to exert to get it moving, or to stop it once it is moving. A heavy motor car requires more braking than a light one. The *weight* of a body is measured by the earth's gravitational attraction on it, but since the weight depends on the mass this is what we actually use. A pair of scales balances the gravitational attraction of the object being weighed against the pull on a standard mass such as a kilogram.

Most peole are now quite familiar with the 'weightlessness' of objects in orbiting space craft. Although scientists always try to make the distinction between mass and weight, they too usually speak of 'weighing' something to find its mass. From now on we shall use whatever word is convenient.

Here is a summary of the complete range of units of mass you will meet, with their symbols and numerical equivalents:

kilogram	kg	1000 g
gram	g	
milligram	mg	0.001 g (1/1000 gram)
microgram	μg	0.001 mg

A printer who does not have the Greek μ will sometimes print mcg for microgram. This is quite wrong and should not be copied. It is better to write the word in full.

The numerical equivalents given are the most useful ones. Although the test that follows will move from one unit to another using decimals if necessary, the important general rule urged upon doctors and pharmacists is to avoid decimal points where possible by writing in smaller units. Instead of 0.25 g it is better to write 250 mg, instead of 0.15 mg, it is better to have 150 μg. As nurses, though, you have to get used to reading quantities however expressed. Refer to the appendix on decimals if you have any difficulty about the unit conversions.

Answers from p. 16.

1.	10 000 m	6.	2360 μm	11.	0.52 cm
2.	0.1 mm	7.	1.723 km	12.	150 mm × 50 mm
3.	150 mm	8.	15 dm	13.	130 mm
4.	1.5 cm	9.	30 nm	14.	21 μm
5.	1.73 m	10.	5200 m	15.	23.5 cm

Now try the test. It is not arranged so that each question follows from the other; you will have to think through each item.

Progress test 2

1. Express 1.4 g in milligrams.
2. Convert 1.8 mg to grams.
3. Convert 1.8 mg to micrograms.
4. How many micrograms are there in half a milligram?
5. Write 1560 g as kilograms.
6. An adult takes three 500 mg aspirin tablets. How many grams is this?
7. Express 500 μg in milligrams.
8. Express 0.25 mg digoxin as a dose in micrograms.
9. How many 250 mg ampicillin capsules should be given for a 1 g dose?
10. What mass is grams is equivalent to 1.75 kg?
11. How many 250 mg tablets of dried aluminium hydroxide gel could be made from each kilogram of bulk stock?
12. A thin wire 1 m long has a mass of 1 g. What is the mass of 5 mm of this wire?
13. Digoxin is also prescribed in doses of 0.125 mg and 0.0625 mg. Express these in micrograms.
14. How many micrograms are there in half a gram?
15. Express 0.002 μg in nanograms.

The answers are given at the foot of p. 20.

MEASURING VOLUME: THE LITRE

The litre is the basic hospital unit of capacity (or volume) of fluid, and is used for measuring both liquids and gases. It is not a separate fundamental unit of the SI system, but it is related to both mass and length. For all practical purposes a litre is that volume of water that weighs one kilogram.

It follows that a thousandth part of a litre weighs a thousandth part of a kilogram — that is

one millilitre of water weighs one gram.

This is a very useful relation indeed.

There are some others which we shall give without further explanation because they rarely concern us in nursing:

1000 litres occupy one cubic metre
1000 litres of water weigh 1000 kg or one 'metric tonne'

Answers from p. 19.

1.	1400 mg	6.	1.5 g	11.	4000
2.	0.0018 g	7.	0.5 mg	12.	5 mg
3.	1800 μg	8.	250 μg	13.	125 μg, 62.5 μg
4.	500	9.	4	14.	500 000 or 5 $\times$ 10^5
5.	1.560 kg	10.	1750 g	15.	2 ng

1   litre occupies one cubic decimetre

1   millilitre occupies one cubic centimetre.

This last relation is very familiar to motorists, who still tend to use the obsolete symbol cc instead of the correct cm^3. They know that a 1985 cc engine is just short of 2 litres. The formal SI definition of a litre is in fact one cubic decimetre, which relates it to the fundamental unit of length.

Look carefully at a few metric containers outside the hospital — bottles of cooking oil, wine, liquid detergent and so on, to give yourself an idea of what a litre is. An ordinary wine bottle will hold three quarters of a litre. Compare them with the measuring vessels you see on the wards.

It is obvious that the litre is a rather large unit for many medical purposes, and the smaller unit in general use is the millilitre, one thousandth of a litre. This is now quite familiar to most people, because the standard spoon for liquid medicines is 5 ml. There is a chance of confusing the symbol l for litre with a 1, reading, for example, 2 l as twenty-one, especially if typed. For this reason some printed texts use an italic or script *l*.

Try to get quite familiar with the millilitre as a unit of measure; it is easily the most important one you will actually have to use in practice. It is not likely that you will ever have to weigh out a dose of a solid drug, but you will often have to measure out a liquid one.

Examine carefully measuring cylinders and the barrels of hypodermic syringes to see how they are calibrated, and try to practise measuring out or taking up various quantities of water. Given any quantity that you are likely to meet in your daily life as a nurse, it is always worthwhile to have a rough idea of how big it is. Many mistakes seem to involve a factor of ten. A measure is given as ten times too much or ten times too small. To an experienced nurse such results should *look* wrong and call for checking.

Although in hospital practice you will not have to deal with units other than the litre and millilitre, countries that already use the metric system often use centilitres:

1 cl = 1/100 litre = 10 ml.

You will often see 70 cl or 75 cl on the labels of wine bottles, and it could appear on any imported liquid products. Some pathology values are given using the decilitre (1 l = 10 dl), but in practice this is usually written as 100 ml. A familiar example often seen in newspaper reports is the 80 mg/100 ml set as a legal limit for blood alcohol in drivers.

Examine a fluid intake and output chart. You will see that liquids taken by mouth and urine excreted are measured in millilitres. A cup of tea, for example, is about 140 ml, and a measuring cylinder used for urine is usually graduated in 100 ml divisions. It is merely a question of both measuring and recording in the one unit, without conversion. Visitors may bring bottles of mineral water and so on for patients on controlled fluid intake; this causes no difficulty since they are now all labelled in litres or millilitres. As part of your training in thinking metric, always look at such labelled bottles and try to judge their contents.

One very important measure arises in connection with blood transfusions, intravenous drips and the like. Here the total necessary intake in 24 hours is given in litres. Setting up and monitoring drips is not to be learnt from a book on SI, but clearly accurate measurement is involved. This is done by using, as part of the apparatus, a visual drip chamber, through which the liquid falls in drops from a standard orifice. The size of the orifice varies with the manufacturer of the apparatus, but typical measures would be:

30 drops per minute = 2 litres/24 hours
45 drops per minute = 3 litres/24 hours.

Note that 24 hours is used, not the word 'day', which could be confused with 12 hours.

Monitoring is by counting the drops over a one minute interval and adjusting the flow as needed. Actual measurement is not called for; the drop rates would be provided with the apparatus. They also depend on the liquid infused, since blood forms larger drops than solutions in water.

A modification of this drops per minute over a 24-hour administration is sometime used for special purposes such as in intensive care baby units, where comparatively small amounts of liquid may need to be administered intravenously over a shorter period. Here the dose is regulated by a burette which allows small drops, often called 'microdrops' (although the prefix has nothing to do with SI) to flow at, say, 60 drops per millilitre. The burette chamber is itself calibrated and is usually filled, intermittently, with a measured amount from the upper litre bag which is then closed off. This quantity is then delivered over the prescribed time period as checked by a drop count.

As before, the nurse responsible does not measure, but counts. Yet another use of drop counts is given in the example about eye drops in Progress Test 3.

Apart from direct measurement, the ml is extensively used in calculating the correct strengths and dosages of drugs dissolved in liquids, as syrups or for purposes of injections. This is an important procedure whose failure will lead to giving the wrong dose. Such solutions are made up so that each millilitre contains a stated weight (or mass) of the active drug. For example, digoxin elixir (0.05 mg/ml) is used in paediatrics. Each millilitre of the elixir contains 0.05 mg of digoxin, so a prescribed dose of 0.1 mg would require 2 ml to be given.

Here is a short test before we go on to some calculations:

1. Write 2 l as millilitres.
2. Express 250 ml as litres.
3. How many 50 ml containers could be filled from 1½ litres of bulk solution?
4. How many millitres of a 25 mg/ml solution will give a dose of 75 mg?
5. A patient drinks two cups of tea (140 ml each) and a bottle of tonic water labelled 240 ml (24 cl). How much liquid is this? What would be its weight? (Take it as that of pure water.)

The answers are at the foot of p. 24.

For liquid drugs as dispensed for supply to the public, the procedure, as far as this is possible, is to make up each prescription so that the required dose is contained in one or more 5 ml standard medicine spoons. This makes the administration in the home simpler and safer.

In a hospital, particularly where injections need to be given from sterile solutions made up in sealed ampoules, such procedures are not always possible, and inevitably correct dosage may sometimes call for calculations. These are simple to perform, but failure to get the right answer can obviously lead to serious consequences.

Many hospitals, of course, have nurses working in pairs on drug rounds to reduce as far as possible, even if they cannot actually eliminate, the probability of error. Certainly you should get your calculation checked before administering the dose.

It is also true that modern presentation of drugs has reduced calculation to a minimum. Drugs for injection are supplied in a range of strengths, and it should be only a matter of choosing the correct one dose ampoule.

Ampoules will be clearly labelled with the dose and the liquid contents. Examples would be:

Digoxin   0.5 mg/2 ml

Atropine   600 µg/ml

There ought not to be any exceptions to this, but one must be prepared for emergencies. Sooner or later the correct ampoule may not be available, and then calculation is needed to get the required amount.

The arithmetic is simple. For a one dose ampoule it is:

$$\text{Fraction to use} = \frac{\text{number of milligrams required}}{\text{number of milligrams available}}$$

Here is an example set out in full:

A 10 mg dose of morphine is to be injected, but the only available ampoule contains 1 ml of strength 15 mg/ml. How much should be taken?

$$
\begin{aligned}
\text{Fraction} &= \frac{\text{milligrams required}}{\text{milligrams available}} \\
&= \frac{10}{15} \\
&= \frac{2}{3}
\end{aligned}
$$

You therefore inject 2/3 of the ampoule or 0.66 ml. See Appendix 2 if you are not sure of this decimal equivalent. Learning to fill a syringe from an ampoule will be part of your training. You may well find that the 1 ml ampoule contains fractionally more than 1 ml, so that the syringe can be filled accurately to 1 ml using the graduations on the barrel. The rest of the solution is discarded. All this is a matter for demonstration and practice.

Here is one more example:

A 1 ml ampoule of pethidine contains 50 mg/ml. What fraction of a millilitre is required for a 20 mg dose?

_____

Answers from p. 23.

  1. 2000 ml   4. 3 ml
  2. 0.25 l   5. 520 ml, 520 g
  3. 30

$$\text{Fraction} = \frac{20}{50}$$
$$= \frac{2}{5}$$

Since 2/5 = 0.4 (see Appendix 2 if you are not sure) the amount to be administered is 0.4 ml.

We want to make it clear that the need for such calculations should be the exception rather than the rule, but you will want to be ready for them should they arise.

Try a few examples before reading on. They are for practice only and do not refer to any specific drug.

What fraction of an ampoule is needed for the following? Express your result both as an ordinary fraction and a decimal.
1. A dose of 2 mg from a 1 ml ampoule of strength 5 mg/ml.
2. A dose of 40 μg from a 1 ml ampoule of strength 100 μg/ml
3. A dose of 0.4 mg from a 2 ml ampoule of strength 0.5 mg/2 ml.

The answers are at the foot of p. 26.

Some drugs are supplied in multidose rubber capped or glass stoppered containers which state the solution strength on the label. The calculation is similar to that already discussed.

If we call the number of milligrams per millilitre in the vial the *strength*, we get

$$\text{number of millilitres administered} = \frac{\text{dose required}}{\text{strength available}}$$

Since you are calculating the number of millilitres to administer you should, strictly speaking, think of dividing the *number* of milligrams required by the *number* of milligrams available in the ampoule, but the easiest way of remembering what you have to do is the form given. You could even reduce it to

$$\frac{\text{required}}{\text{available}}$$

as long as you realize that this is only a mnemonic to help you arrive at the correct result.

Example

What quantity of solution is required for an injection of 75 mg of cortisone if the multidose container is of strength 25 mg/ml?

Dose required	= 75 mg
Strength	= 25 mg/ml
Number of millilitres	= $\dfrac{75}{25}$
	= 3

This is the quantity injected.

Sometimes the active material is measured in international biological units (i.u.) rather than by weight. The calculations go in the same way.

Example

A patient requires 12 500 units of heparin. How much should be drawn from a multidose vial of strength 5000 i.u./ml?

Required	= 12 500 units
Available	5000 units/ml
Number of millilitres withdrawn	= $\dfrac{12\ 500}{5000}$
	= 2.5

So 2.5 ml are withdrawn. A calculation such as this is best checked by multiplication. Check that 5000 × 2.5 brings you back to 12 500. Such calculations are not just exercises in mathematics; they could be a matter of life and death.

Do note that the strengths available may vary considerably. Heparin, for

---

Answers from p. 25.
1. 2/5 of 1 ml = 0.4 ml
2. 40/100 of 1 ml = 0.4 ml
3. 4/5 of 2 ml = 1.6 ml

These answers are fractions of an ampoule, but are also given in millilitres since we have ampoules of known capacity.

example, if in multidose containers, may be 5000 units/ml or 25 000 units/ml. Insulin is usually supplied in 10 ml vials of strengths 20, 40 or 80 units/ml. The various strengths are often colour-coded but this code varies from supplier to supplier. The strengths of such drugs are chosen so that as far as possible only one or a whole number of millilitres need be withdrawn if the correct vial is used. The calculation just given, for a dose of 2.5 ml, should be an exception rather than a rule.

Avoidable mathematics is always a possible source of error, but if it cannot be avoided it is important that you check the strength you are dealing with as well as any calculations you do. Ideally, for the greatest possible safety, you should be able to select tablets and solutions that do not require paper and pencil calculations, but you must nevertheless be able to cope with such arithmetic as the supplies available make necessary. Having two people working together is always an advantage if it can be done.

Sometimes two stages of calculation are needed. Infants with heart conditions are prescribed digoxin, if this is indicated, by body weight, for example with a dosage of 0.025 mg/kg taken from a paediatric elixir containing 0.05 mg/l. The first stage in this calculation would always be done by the doctor writing the prescription, but it is as well to know what is needed. The example shows the two stages:

An infant weighs 4 kg and a dose of 0.025 mg/kg body weight is indicated. How many millilitres should be administered from an elixir containing 0.05 mg/ml?

First stage

Dose rate	= 0.025 mg/kg
Body weight	= 4 kg
Prescribed dose	= (0.025 × 4) mg
	= 0.1 mg

Second stage

$$\frac{\text{Required dose}}{\text{strength available}} = \frac{0.1}{0.05}$$
$$= 2 \, (\text{ml})$$

In this example, as in many others, decimals can be avoided by using smaller units — in this case the microgram. The dose could be given as 25 μg/kg, the elixir as 50 μg/ml

Setting the example out exactly as before:

Dose rate $\qquad$ = 25 μg/kg
Body weight $\qquad$ = 4 kg
Prescribed dose $\qquad$ = (25 × 4) μg
$\qquad\qquad\qquad$ = 100 μg

$$\frac{\text{Required dose}}{\text{Strength available}} = \frac{100}{50}$$

$$= 2\,\text{ml}$$

and so 2 ml are administered, as before.

When you are used to doing these calculations there is, of course, no need to set out each one in full. Remember, though, that when given a prescription it is your responsibility to measure out the correct dose. You will see from the example above that though one does not have to weigh drugs directly in micrograms, these can be very useful for calculation and you should always be able to convert to and from this tiny unit. If in doubt, get your result checked. Uncertainty, remember, is likely to cause less harm than misplaced confidence.

IMPORTANT NOTE

Every nurse will hear of fatalities caused by an overdose of dangerous drugs, because of wrong prescription or mistakes in calculating and measuring dosage. Since such mistakes, if they occur, are often associated with misreading or miscalculating decimal quantities, the authors would strongly support a decision always to prescribe drugs such as digoxin in micrograms. The calculation in the second example is clearly less liable to error.

Progress test 3

1. What is the weight of 250 ml of water?
2. A 1500 unit dose is required from a 2500 unit/ml ampoule. How much, in ml, is required?
3. How many millilitres of a 0.05 mg/ml elixir would you administer to a child requiring a dose of 0.20 mg?
4. Express 1½ litres in centilitres.
5. Write these fractions of a litre in millilitres:
   ¾, ½, 1/5.

6. A healthy baby weighs 3.5 kg at the end of the second week and gains about 200 g/week. What will be the baby's approximate weight at the end of the sixth week?

7. The maximum daily made up milk requirement for a normal baby artificially fed is about 200 ml/kg each day. What is the maximum daily requirement for a baby weighing 4.5 kg?

8. How much is to be given at each feed if the baby of question seven is fed five times a day?

9. How much of digoxin elixir should be withdrawn from a solution of strength 0.05 mg/ml for a dose of 0.03 mg?

10. Express these solution strengths in μg/ml:
    a) 0.25 mg/ml   b) 250 mg/l   c) 0.05 mg/ml.

11. During a day a patient drinks 5 cups of tea or cocoa (140 ml each), has tablets three times a day taken each time with 50 ml of water, and one glass of water (250 ml). Urine collection is 250 ml, 200 ml, 155 ml, 160 ml, 200 ml. What are the intake and output totals?

12. A bath prepared for a patient contained 110 l of water. What would this water weigh?

13. How many days would a 10 ml eye dropper bottle last if one drop has to be placed in each eye three times a day, and there are 15 drops to the millitre?

14. If stock digoxin tablets contain 0.0625 mg, how many should be given for a dose of 0.125 mg?

The answers are at the foot of p. 30.

SECTION 4

MEASURING PRESSURE: THE PASCAL

If you blow up a toy balloon, it expands because of the pressure of the air inside, and if there is a hole in it, the air will stream out, impelled by this internal pressure. Gases and liquids under pressures that need to be measured have played an important part in science and technology, and there grew up many different ways of measuring this quantity, using units derived in different ways.

The SI unit of pressure is called the pascal, after the French mathematician Pascal, but it has not yet been fully adopted, either by hospitals or in the wide range of industrial measurements. Because the pascal is related to the other SI units in a way that simplifies calculations, it is likely to be only a matter of time before it is generally adopted in hospitals, and it is already the standard pressure

---

---

unit used in pathology departments. The symbol for pascal is Pa (note the capital letter) and the commonest unit is the kilopascal, kPa, or one thousand pascals.

The commonest pressure measurement you will undertake is that of the blood, the pressure produced by the pumping action of the heart. This is measured with an instrument, the sphygmomanometer, which in its original form balanced the pressure of the blood against that produced by a column of the very heavy liquid metal mercury (almost twice as heavy, bulk for bulk, as cast iron). For this reason blood pressure was and still is recorded directly in millimetres of mercury, mmHg, the height of the column of mercury (chemical symbol Hg, from the old name *hydrargarium* — liquid silver) measured in millimetres. Some modern instruments have a pointer on a dial instead of a mercury column, and are easier to read.

Instruction and practice in the actual use of the sphygmomanometer will come early on in any course. What we are concerned with here are the units of pressure that it shows on its scale. If it has a mercury tube this will be graduated in millimetres from zero to 300, so that you read off directly the pressure in mmHg. The dial type will have its scale similarly marked, although it may have a double scale with one graduated in kilopascals, the other in mmHg.

Do note that you will not have to convert from millimetres of mercury to pascals or kilopascals. If in the future the SI unit is generally used, it will merely be a matter of replacing the scale. The actual conversion is:

$$\text{Pressure in kilopascals} = \frac{\text{Pressure in mmHg}}{7.5}$$

Example: What is the maximum on the scale in kilopascals?

$$\text{Reading} = \frac{300}{7.5} \text{ kPa}$$
$$= 40 \text{ kPa}$$

so that 300 mmHg is equal to 40 kPa.

All that you will need in practice is to read from a scale running from 0 – 40 kPa instead of 0 – 300 mmHg. It will help if you look at the diagram showing the two scales as given in Appendix 3.

Normal systolic pressures run from about 14 kPa (100 mmHg) for babies to

20 kPa (150 mmHg) for middle-aged adults, but much higher or lower readings may be obtained in abnormal or special conditions.

Pressure measurements are also used in hospitals for gases such as oxygen or nitrous oxide in cylinders, and also for recording the equivalent pressure of gases present in the blood. Using modern methods of analysis, this is a convenient way for a laboratory worker to find out how much oxygen and carbon dioxide is held by the blood. Carbon dioxide in arterial blood, for example, is usually between 5 and 6 kPa. You will find references to such measurements in your textbooks, and you must at least understand what is meant. An experienced nurse working in an intensive care unit would certainly need to work with these measures.

Test

1. Use the diagram of Appendix 3 to convert the following pressures to kilopascals:
   90 mmHg,   120 mmHg,   210 mmHg.
2. Calculate these pressures as kilopascals:
   140 mmHg,   198 mmHg,   123 mmHg.

The answers are at the foot of p. 34.

This test is given as an exercise only: you are unlikely to need conversion by calculation in the course of your duties. Hospitals are now in the transition period, and eventually sphygmomanometers will be directly calibrated in kilopascals if the change is made at some future date. In fact mmHg is such a convenient unit that it may never be replaced in measuring blood pressures.

SECTION 5

MEASURING ENERGY: THE JOULE

The actual *measurement* of energy is a highly technical procedure and is of no immediate professional concern to nurses. The concept of energy and the exchange of energy, however, is of vital importance to all biological studies of sickness or of health, and you will want to understand them. Any change of physical state, of motion, of temperature, of chemical composition — any change whatever that can actually be seen or heard or detected in some way — is accompanied by an exchange of energy. When you pay your electricity bill you are actually paying for the energy you use to heat your house and drive your domestic appliances. All forms of energy are interchangeable. The power station turns the heat energy of burning coal into the mechanical energy of the steam turbines. This in turn produces electrical energy which is used in our homes to produce heat or light or mechanical energy.

For the human being, as for all animals, the source of energy is food. The control of energy intake as food is an important part of the treatment of patients, and this is the job of the dietician. You will often hear discussion of energy requirements in sickness or health, and you will wish to follow them.

At one time the energy of food was measured in heat units called 'great calories' or 'Calories' with an initial capital. These are still used in the older textbooks when referring to diet, but the international unit that is gradually replacing the diet calorie is called the joule (after an English scientist J.P. Joule). The symbol is J, and the only form you are likely to meet is kJ, the kilojoule or 1000 J. It is a derived unit of the SI system, and like the calorie it is not

33

easy to measure; it is a task for the laboratory and not the hospital kitchen. A kilojoule is the energy used by a one kilowatt electric heater in just one second.

But you will need to know about the energy requirements of your patients and the way in which various foods contribute to this. During the period of transition you will see both units in use, but try to remember the SI form. One diet calorie or Calorie is about 4.2 kJ, although a more useful relation is:

$$1000 \text{ diet calories} = 4200 \text{ kJ}$$

This relation is not exact, but neither is the calculation of food energy. The figures are always 'rounded off', and a diet would be given as 1500 Calories or 6300 kJ, not as, for example, 1487 Calories or its 'exact' equivalent 6224.58 kJ.

You will have to be ready to deal with the difficulties of transition, since you may well have to explain diet sheets to patients. Although most patients are unlikely to know what a diet calorie actually is, they are familiar with the word and see it continually in use in magazines and newspaper articles: they are not puzzled if told they must not exceed 2100 calories per day, but they may refuse to try to understand 8600 kJ. For the rough translation of dietary energy requirements divide the kilojoule value by four to get an estimate in diet calories sufficiently close for culinary purposes. Otherwise you can use a twin scale and read off the equivalents directly, as in Appendix 3.

Since the gram is rather small for a food portion and the kilogram rather large, it is usual to give the energy value of foods in centigram units, but these are always written as 100 g rather than 1 cg. Here are a few examples, which must be taken as approximate, except for 'pure' foodstuffs like sugar or starch:

Meat	450 kJ/100 g
Bread	1000 kJ/100 g
Sugar	1650 kJ/100 g
Fish	320 kJ/100 g

Answers from p. 32.
1. 12.0 kPa,   16.0 kPa,   28 kPa
2. 18.7 kPa,   26.4 kPa,   16.4 kPa

For a rough calculation of diet in terms of its main energy constituents you can take the values:

Proteins	1700 kJ/100 g
Fats	3800 kJ/100 g
Carbohydrates	1600 kJ/100 g

These are average values for classes of substances. There are many different kinds of fat, protein and carbohydrate, and a natural food such as meat contains them in very varying proportions. This is why 'exact' values cannot be given and only 'rounded' figures have practical value for ordinary dietetic purposes. Do remember that a food does not 'contain' calories or kilojoules: energy is not a food substance which is bad for the obese!

The kilojoule merely measures the total amount of energy available if the food is used or burnt up by the body. Unused energy is either converted into heat and sweated off or, among the less fortunate, stored as the chemical energy in excess fat.

Any use you make of the units of pressure and energy will not involve you, at least in your work as a nurse, in calculations.

This Progress Test reviews all the units used so far.

Progress Test 4

1. Express 1.46 l as millilitres.
2. Diet for an adult should contain about 9 mg iron per day. How many micrograms is this?
3. A low-sodium diet for cardiac disease permits 1500 mg intake per day. How many grams is this?
4. A high protein diet is prescribed at the rate of 1.5 g/kg per day. What weight of protein should a 70 kg adult take each day?
5. Express 1.65 m as centimetres.
6. What is 0.07 mm as micrometres?
7. Express 0.5 mg/ml as grams per litre.
   (Hint: Do this in two stages if necessary — first into g/ml then g/l. Could you have done it more easily?)
8. Correct the following numbers which are printed wrongly:
   1 273.2;   .273;   4,321.
9. Express 2500 diet calories as kilojoules.

10. Express 150 mmHg as kilopascals.
11. Rewrite 0.125 mg/ml as micrograms per millitre.
12. A pharmaceutical company produce ten million antacid tablets a year, each weighing 500 mg. What is the total weight?
13. A hospital corridor is 120 m long. A patient on controlled exercise walks up and down this five times in each direction. What is the total distance walked in kilometres?
14. How many 5 ml doses can be drawn from a stock bottle containing 1 l?
15. Convert 50 μm to millimetres.

Answers are at the bottom of p. 38.

SECTION 6

MEASURING SUBSTANCE: THE MOLE

The mole, like the pascal, is a unit you will continually meet in modern text-books. It is widely used in pathology laboratories, but only the laboratory worker needs to calculate using this unit. It is a measure of the quantity of substance, at first introduced solely for the purposes of laboratory calculations involving the chemical reactions of pure substances. This earlier chemical unit will already be familiar to those students who have done some chemistry as the 'gram-molecule'. This is the molecular weight of a substance in grams. For some purposes scientists need a more sophisticated measure than the early form, and the mole is the modern SI version devised for their use. Unless you actually become a worker in clinical chemistry you can most conveniently think of the mole merely as a renaming of the old unit. Later in your career, or in postregistration training, you may possibly need to use the mole, but it becomes more a matter of learning chemistry and physics than learning SI.

The note that follows may help those who have not done any chemistry, and may be skipped by those who have.

You will know that ordinary substances are either elements or compounds. Elements are composed of atoms, but other substances have their particles made up from atoms. All the particles of any one pure substance are of identical atomic constitution and are called molecules. The 'molecules' of an element will simply be atoms or perhaps pairs of atoms. It follows that all the molecules of any one substance, such as water, have exactly the same mass: that of the constituent atoms. For water (chemical formula, H_2O) this is 18 units, since it is composed of two hydrogen atoms each of one unit in mass, and one oxygen atom of mass 16 units. The atomic 'unit' is, roughly speaking, the mass of the hydrogen atom.

The mole, for our purposes, is the molecular weight *in grams*. One mole of water weighs 18 g. The alcohol molecule (chemical formula C_2H_5OH) as another example, is made up with two carbon atoms of mass 12 units, six hydrogen and one oxygen, and therefore has a total mass of 46 units. One mole of alcohol, then, weighs 46 g. The importance of the mole for chemistry is that chemical reactions involve whole molecules of the substances concerned. Thus one atom of sodium (mass 23) combines with one of chlorine (mass 35.5) to make a molecule of sodium chloride (or common salt) of mass 58.5. This means that 23 g of sodium will combine with 35.5 g of chlorine, or, in other words, one mole of each will combine to give a mole of salt, weighing 58.5 g.

One result of this is that the various moles of various substances all contain exactly the same number of particles. One atom of sodium with one of chlorine gives one molecule of salt, and 23 g of sodium atoms combine with 35.5 g of chlorine atoms to give 58.5 g of salt molecules: there is exactly the same number of particles in 23 g of sodium as in 58.5 g of salt. This number is very large, although we can easily write it in the notation of p. 10. It is roughly 6×10^{23}, and is called Avogadro's number.

The important point to grasp is that the mole is a measure chosen for describing chemical processes, and varies in actual weight from one substance to the next. You cannot have a measure calibrated in moles. You must first know the molecular weight, and then weigh out that number of grams.

This is why the mole is not used for the complex protein substances found in living tissue; their molecules are so large and complicated that their exact mass is not known. Thus you can measure the glucose in blood serum in moles per litre

---

Answers from p. 36.

1. 1460 ml	6. 70 μm	11. 125 μg/ml
2. 9000 μg	7. 0.5 g/l	12. 5000 kg
3. 1.5g	8. 1273.2,	13. 1.2 km
	0.273,	
4. 105 g	4321	14. 200
5. 165 cm	9. 10 500 kJ	15. 0.05 mm
	10. 20 kP	

Note the answer to 7. It is not really a 'catch question', although you may have worked it out. Since *both* units are to be multiplied by 1000 the proportion is the same: 0.5 mg/ml = 0.5 g/l. Exactly the same thing happens in reverse, and 27 mg/l = 27 μg/ml.

(actually it is from 3 to about 8 millimoles per litre), but albumin can only be measured in grams per litre. This is because glucose has a known molecular weight (180) but albumin is a complex protein of unknown molecular weight.

You now have enough information to be able to follow pathology laboratory results or biochemical report forms which may need to be filed with or transferred to patients' notes. Look at some of these forms, which may show the normal ranges or reference values.

It should be clear from our simplified account of the mole as molecular mass in grams that it measures the amount of substance present. It is a useful laboratory alternative to expressing content by weight. By and large the clinical chemist uses mmol/l instead of mg/100 ml. You, as a nurse, will not usually need to convert from one to the other, but perhaps you would like the formula for reference:

$$\text{Concentration in mmol/l} = \frac{\text{Concentration in mg/100 ml} \times 10}{\text{molecular weight of substance}}$$

As long as you realize that mg/100 ml, g/l, mmol/l and so on are different ways of measuring the concentration of substances dissolved in the body fluids, and can see the importance of normal or reference values in health, or departure from them in disease, you will have done enough for your work as a nurse. You will see the mole in use on drip bags of normal saline, of capacity 500 ml or 1000 ml. These are now labelled with the strength expressed both as a percentage and in millimoles of salt (sodium chloride, NaCl) per litre of solution. Sometimes the Na and Cl are given separately. Solutions added in small quantities to intravenous fluid may use a 10 ml unit. You will often see potassium chloride, KCl, made up for this purpose at a strength of 15 mmol/10 ml.

Here is a test. If you can do this you will have done more than you are likely to need.

Test

1. A molecule of iron weighs more than a molecule of calcium. If you have a mole of each, which weighs the most?
2. The molecular weight of common salt (sodium chloride) is 58.5. What is the weight of a mole of salt?
3. Why is the albumin content of blood serum expressed in g/l and not mol/l?

4. A biochemical report on a patient's serum albumin gives 42 g/l. How much is this in g/100 ml?
5. A mole of glucose weighs 180 g. What is its molecular weight?
6. The excreted calcium in urine is usually measured in mmol/24 h. If the total volume of urine is 24 h in 1500 ml and the calcium content is 8 mmol/l, what is the total calcium?
7. What must be known before one can make up a solution of a substance to a concentration given in mol/l?
8. A molecule of urea contains one carbon, one oxygen, two nitrogen and four hydrogen atoms. The masses of the atoms are 12, 16, 14 and 1 respectively in atomic units. What is the weight of 1 mole of urea?
9. If a substance, such as iodine, is present in the blood in such small quantities that even the micromole is too big a unit, what unit could be used? Write 0.32 μmol/l in a unit that avoids decimal points.
10. A carbon atom (mass 12) combines with two atoms of oxygen (mass 16) to form carbon dioxide. What weight of oxygen is required to burn up completely 12 g of carbon? How much carbon dioxide is produced (in moles)?

Answers given at the foot of p. 42.

SECTION 7

MEASURING TEMPERATURE: THE DEGREE CELSIUS

To 'have a temperature' is universally recognized as a symptom of illness. The thermometer is an instrument widely known and understood by most people. Since the normal range of body temperature is narrow, and since quite small changes are significant, the clinical thermometer is more accurate and finely calibrated than the ordinary domestic thermometer. You will, of course, learn about its construction and use during your training, and you may well come to use the newer non-mercury thermometers now available. What matters here is that you become familiar with the unit of measurement. Thermometry has a long history and there have been many different scales.

SI has a special unit of temperature called the kelvin, but it has taken over, for ordinary use, the original Celsius scale already internationally recognized. On this scale water freezes at zero units and boils at 100. The intervening span of temperature is divided into 100 equal parts called degrees Celsius, symbol °C. These units are often called Centigrade degrees in England, but the word is not used in SI since it means something quite different in many countries, where it is, or was, a measure of angle. It is, however, heard frequently in England and will no doubt survive for many years.

Unfortunately, the United Kingdom and the United States also adopted the more complicated 18th century Fahrenheit scale at which water freezes at 32° and boils at 212°. This is better ignored in your professional work. Do not attempt conversions, but become quite familiar with normal ranges expressed in the correct form, as the clinical thermometer measures them. You should learn the usual body ranges as well as a few other reference values useful in hospital.

Range of clinical thermometer (normal)		35°C – 42°C
	(low range)	28°C – 40°C
Body temperatures		
Subnormal		below 36.5°C
Normal range		36.5°C – 37.5°C
Above normal — slight		not above 38.5°C
— moderate		not above 39.5°C
— high		not above 40.5°C
— very high		above 40.5°C
Water freezes		0°C
Water boils		100°C
Cool room		15°C
Warm room		20°C
Hot room		25°C
Cold bath		15°C
Tepid bath		30°C
Hot bath		40°C

Although, ideally, you should never convert from Celsius to Fahrenheit you may still find the latter in use in older text or reference books. The simplest and safest way to get the required values is to use a double scale as given in Appendix 3.

Answers from p. 40.

1. The mole of iron
2. 58.5 g
3. Because it is of uncertain molecular weight
4. 4.2 g
5. 180
6. 12 mmol/24 h
7. Its molecular weight
8. 60 g
9. The nanomole, 320 nmol/l
10. 32 g. One mole.

Progress Test 5

This test includes questions on every section of the book. Rewrite the following measures in the units given:

1. 53 ml in litres
2. The sum of 426 ml, 200 ml and 746 ml in litres
3. 250 μm as millimetres
4. 0.75 mg as micrograms
5. 15.3 mmol/100 ml as millimoles per litre
6. 191 cm as metres
7. 231 mm as centimetres
8. 75 cl as litres
9. 0.002 g as milligrams
10. 450 μg as milligrams.

Use the double scale diagrams to make the following conversions for reference purposes:

11. 101°F as degrees Celsius
12. 1050 kJ as dietetic calories
13. 135 mmHg as kilopascals
14. 7 mmol/l of serum glucose to mg/100 ml
15. 90 mg/100 l of serum glucose to mmol/l.

Answers at the foot of p. 45.

You have now met all the units of measure required for nursing purposes, and have been introduced to those others you will meet in use during your professional studies. You do, however, need more than theoretical knowledge, and full competence in clinical measurement can only come as the result of repeated practice.

SUMMARY

Here is a final list of all the SI units you will need arranged in two groups.

Units for frequent or occasional use, which may sometimes call for calculations or conversion from one unit to another

Length	kilometre	1 km	=	1000 m
	metre			
	(decimetre)	1 m	=	10 dm
	centimetre	1 m	=	100 cm
	millimetre	1 m	=	1000 mm
	micrometre	1 μm	=	10^{-6} m
Mass	kilogram	1 kg	=	1000 g
	gram			
	milligram	1 g	=	1000 mg
	microgram	1 μg	=	10^{-6} g
	(nanogram)	1 ng	=	10^{-9} g
Capacity	litre			
	(centilitre)	1 l	=	10 cl
	millilitre	1 l	=	1000 ml

SI also includes the usual measures of time: seconds, minutes, hours.

Units to be used for measurement or reference only, and not normally calling for calculation by nursing staff

Temperature	degree Celsius (or Centigrade)		
Pressure	kilopascal (also millimetres of mercury)	1 kP	= 1000 P
Energy	kilojoule	1 kJ	= 1000 J
Substance	mole millimole	1 mol	= 1000 mmol

A complete list of the multiplying prefixes of SI is given, for reference only, in Appendix 1.

If you began by trying the Diagnostic Test given as Appendix 4, and found that you had difficulty with it, try it again now that you have finished the book. Your work will have been successful if you can complete the test. If you can answer the questions (even if here and there you have to refer back to the text), you will certainly be able to cope with the system of measurement that is now standard in hospitals throughout the world.

Answers from p. 43.

1. 0.053 l
2. 1.372 l
3. 0.25 mm
4. 750 μg
5. 153 mmol/l
6. 1.91 m
7. 23.1 cm
8. 0.75 l
9. 2 mg
10. 0.45 mg
11. 39°C
12. 250 Calories
13. 18 kPa
14. 126 mg/100 ml
15. 5 mmol/l

THE MULTIPLYING PREFIXES IN SI

Prefix	Symbol	Value
tera-	T	1 000 000 000 000 or 10^{12}
giga-	G	1 000 000 000 or 10^9
mega-	M	1 000 000 or 10^6
kilo-	k	1000
hecto-	h	100
deca-	da	10
deci-	d	0.1 (1/10)
centi-	c	0.01 (1/100)
milli-	m	0.001 (1/1000)
micro-	μ	0.000 001 (1/1 000 000) or 10^{-6}
nano-	n	0.000 000 001 or 10^{-9}
pico-	p	0.000 000 000 001 or 10^{-12}
femto-	f	10^{-15}
atto-	a	10^{-18}

The important four are printed in bold type: these are the ones in everyday clinical use. The prefix symbols T, G and M are the only ones written as capitals. The symbol for micro- is the Greek letter μ pronounced *mu*. It is, however, read as *micro*. The prefix symbols are always written before the unit symbols without a space, as in the examples throughout the book.

APPENDIX 2

THE USE OF DECIMALS

Those responsible for professional training can reasonably be expected to include in their courses any work with measure or mathematics that is not in general use among laymen. Unfortunately they often have to do more. Many entrants to the nursing profession, who should be able to cope with simple general calculations involving decimals, find that their skills, when called for, are embarrassingly rusty. This group may well include some who are now reading this. It is, one hopes, only a question of disuse: all schools will surely have steered their pupils at some time through a course of decimal fractions.

This appendix is intended for rapid revision. It is a reminder of what you ought to have learnt at some time in the past. If the diagnosis is more than forgetfulness and lack of practice, then the treatment calls for more than a few pages added to a book such as this, which sets out to *use* but does not expect to *teach* decimal calculations. You should consult your tutors if what follows is insufficient to reactivate your forgotten skill. Processes discussed will not go beyond what you will actually need to use.

The decimal notation: addition and subtraction

You will already know that in any multidigit number, such as 435, the three digits have quite different values. The number is read as four hundred and thirty five: the digit 4 counts hundreds, the digit 3 tens and the digit 5 units or ones. In adding numbers the columns of units, tens, hundreds and so on must be kept distinct, so that tens are added only to tens and so on:

	607	not	607
	22		22
	540		540
	3		3
	1171		1397

The mistake looks obvious in the example, but the sum of long columns of carelessly written figures is often in error because of such misreading of position. You will also know that the zeros in 607 and 540 mark the 'empty' space, which if merely left vacant would certainly lead to errors in calculation. You will also realize that since the sum of the units column in the example is 12, only the 2 is entered. The digit 1 here stands for one ten, and is therefore taken as a carrying figure to the next column.

The first paragraph was simply a reminder, and it is taken for granted that you can add and subtract whole numbers. The decimal, or decimal fraction, is a device for recording parts of wholes. A length may be 16 m or 17 m exactly, but is quite likely to be something in between. As a first step, the metre is thought of as divided into ten parts or tenths. The length required could then be 16 7/10, perhaps exactly. In the decimal notation this is written as 16.7. Here a new column has been added to the tens and units to record *tenths*, and the decimal point is merely a separator to show us where the units end and the tenths begin. Use of decimal fractions permits addition and subtraction to be done in columns exactly as for whole numbers, as long as the tenths are kept in their own vertical line

	16.7
3.2	13.2
5.6	25.4
8.8	55.3

In the second example the column of tenths add up to 13/10 which is 1 3/10. Since this is written 1.3 in the decimal notation we can record the 3 in the tenths column and 'carry' the one to the units.

The result of all this is that, as long as you keep all the digits in the correct column, with the decimal point as separator, addition and subtraction is done with decimal fractions exactly as with whole numbers. There are two matters to note. The first, important today because there is so much international exchange, is that most non-English speaking countries use a *comma* instead of a point. A German drug house would use 2,5 mg rather than 2.5 mg. The second, very important indeed, is that since the points or commas are easily missed in reading, a decimal fraction without any units figure ALWAYS begins with a zero. It is 0.5 g not .5 g (or 0,5 g not ,5 g). In this way you are less likely to make a mistake if you need to add, for example 6 and 52 and 0.3. The zero helps you keep the digits in their correct position, like this

$$
\begin{array}{r}
6 \\
52 \\
0.3 \\
\hline
58.3 \\
\hline
\end{array}
$$

Sometimes in such cases 6 will be written as 6.0, which is another hint that a tenths column is being used.

If the measure 16 7/10 m or 16.7 m is still not close enough, the next step is to measure the excess length in hundredths, and add one more column:

$$16.73$$

This means sixteen plus 7/10 plus 3/100. The column addition is done as before, but it is now necessary to use *two* zeros if only hundredths are present. Two hundredths of a metre is written 0.02 m, although you will realize that you can avoid the decimal altogether by writing 2 cm. It should be clear that greater accuracy, if needed, can be got by using one more column and working in thousandths. The following diagram, showing part of a magnified scale, may help to fix the meaning of decimal places.

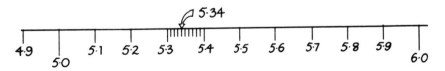

5·34 on a decimal scale.

Do these for practice:

1.   47.26
                0.37
                0.02
                _____

                _____

2.   23
                6.4
                5
                2.5
                _____

                _____

3.   Write 2375 mm as a decimal of a metre.
4.   Write 0.027 mg without decimals.
5.   12.96
              − 1.32
                _____

                _____

6.   Align these in a column and add
                42, 0.03, 1.06, 21
7.   0.002,   4,   3.5,   0.15
8.   12.34
              − 9.76
                _____

                _____

9.   4.326
                0.025
                1.312
                _____

                _____

10.   5.213
              − 1.735

                _____

                _____

The answers are at the foot of p. 52.

Multiplication and division

The multiplication and division of decimal quantities over the wide range of values called for by scientific computations does present problems. Few of these calculations are needed in nursing practice, and this appendix is concerned only with the processes called for by the text of this book. As before (see p. 48) it is assumed that the student can multiply and divide with whole numbers. For the purposes of putting SI units to use you need only to multiply or divide decimal quantities by ten, a hundred or a thousand, or by one digit integers. Conversion, which you as a nurse will not normally do, may call for multiplication or division by decimals such as 4.2 (see p. 56), but it is quicker and much safer to use a double scale as given in Appendix 3. You may also need to express a simple fraction such as 2/5 as a decimal. The appendix will discuss nothing beyond this point.

Multiplication and division by ten

Since we count in units, ten, hundreds and so on multiplication of any number by ten follows the same pattern. Ten lots of three is thirty, ten lots of nine is ninety, and ten lots of a tenth is one unit. So we get:

$$
\begin{array}{ccc}
4 & 9 & 0.1 \\
\times\ 10 & \times\ 10 & \times\ 10 \\
\hline
40 & 90 & 1.0 \\
\hline
\end{array}
$$

In each example the digit moves to the next column on the left, leaving an empty column to be filled by a zero. There is no need to write the zero in the third example, but it has been put in to draw attention to the shift that has taken place. The decimal point itself does not move, and needs to be left where it is to mark the separation of units from tenths. Once again, decimals behave exactly like whole numbers. Students may have difficulty with them because they may have been given confusing 'rules' at school which treat decimals differently from whole numbers — usually at the risk of getting digits in the wrong columns.

Multiplication by 100 or 1000 merely involves an extra shift. One hundred lots of nine is nine hundred, one hundred lots of 1/100 is a unit, one hundred lots of 1/10 is ten units. So we have:

9	3.2	0.27
× 100	× 100	× 100
900	320.0	27.0

with each digit working two places to the left this time.

Multiplication by 1000 moves the digits three places, so that a number such as 0.025 × 1000 becomes 25. It is not, of course necessary to write 25.000, but it might help if you think of the empty columns, especially if you are writing figures down one under the other. Even if you are not adding them up, keep the digits aligned as they are in a properly printed book:

$$296$$
$$1.23$$
$$40$$
$$3$$

Division by 10, 100 or 1000 goes in the opposite direction. On dividing by ten each hundred becomes a ten, each unit a tenth, each tenth a hundredth, and so on:

$$1.63 \div 10 = 0.163$$
$$0.01 \div 10 = 0.001$$

That is, the digits shift one place to the right. Similarly for division by 100 or 1000, the digits shift 2 or 3 places to the right, leaving the decimal separator where it is.

Since conversion from one SI unit to any larger or smaller units involves

---

Answers from p. 50.

1.	47.65	6.	64.09
2.	36.9	7.	7.652
3.	2.375 m	8.	2.58
4.	27 μg	9.	5.663
5.	11.64	10.	3.478

only multiplication or division by tens, hundreds etc., what has been said so far covers the bulk of daily requirements.

Do the following calculations which are like those needed in converting the basic SI units into larger or smaller units:

1. 1.25×10
2. 0.01×1000
3. $2.4 \div 10$
4. $23 \div 1000$
5. 0.001×1000
6. 5.6×100
7. $223 \div 100$

8. $247 \div 10$
9. 12.3×100
10. $5 \div 100$
11. 0.025×1000
12. 0.03×1000
13. 0.45×10
14. 0.6×1000
15. 1.01×100

The answers are at the foot of p. 54.

Multiplication and division of decimals by integers

You may need multiplication by numbers other than tens occasionally, division very rarely. For decimals multiplication by an integer (or whole number) proceeds as for whole numbers:

$$
\begin{array}{r}
4.3 \\
\times\ 7 \\
\hline
30.1 \\
\end{array}
\qquad\qquad
\begin{array}{r}
15.05 \\
\times\ 3 \\
\hline
45.15 \\
\end{array}
$$

Seven lots of three tenths is 21 tenths, so you record the one tenth and carry the two units. The digits behave exactly as in ordinary multiplication; all that is needed is to keep the columns in alignment.

Division needs more thought, because you cannot always divide one number exactly into another: $17 \div 5$ is 3 with a remainder of 2. Decimals allow you to carry on the division. If you think of the remainder of 2 as 20 tenths, then *this* number can be divided by 5 since $20 \div 5 = 4$. 20 tenths divided by 5 is 4 tenths. So $17 \div 5 = 3.4$ (or 3 and four tenths). The 'trick' — it is not really a trick, because it only rewrites the figure in decimal form — is to add a decimal point followed by a zero:

$$17 \div 5 = 17.0 \div 5$$
$$= 3.4$$

or
$$
5\ \overline{)\ 17.^20}
$$
$$
3.\ 4
$$

If there is any remainder from the tenths, think of them as hundredths:

$$17 \div 4$$

becomes $\qquad 4 \;\overline{)\; 17.^10^20}$
$$\qquad\qquad\qquad 4.\;2\;5$$

so $\qquad 17 \div 4 = 4.25$

If there are decimal digits already, just go ahead:

$$4.25 \div 5$$
$$5 \;\overline{)\; 4.^42^25}$$
$$\qquad 0.\;8\;5$$

The calculation is sometimes useful for turning fractions to decimals (see p. 24).

Example: Write 2/5 as a decimal
Here we need to divide 2 by 5, using decimals

$$5 \;\overline{)\; 2.^20}$$
$$\qquad 0.\;4$$

You will not normally need to work with more difficult fractions than this, but if you do, it is done in the same way. Consider 3/7

$$7 \;\overline{)\; 3.^30^20^60^40}$$
$$\qquad 0.\;4\;2\;8\;5$$

Answers from p. 53.

1. 12.5	6. 560	11. 25.0
2. 10.0	7. 2.23	12. 30.0
3. 0.24	8. 24.7	13. 4.5
4. 0.023	9. 1230.0	14. 600.0
5. 1.0	10. 0.05	15. 101.0

A zero has been inserted after decimal points retained in the answers to make clear what has happened to the digits. In practice neither the point nor the zero need be written:

$$0.03 \times 1000 = 30$$
$$2.4 \times 10 = 24$$

Here there is a remainder after each zero you add. This means that 3/7 is never an exact number of tenths, hundredths and so on, but if you were actually measuring something the discrepancy is too small to worry about.

The fraction/decimal calculations likely to arise in nursing are so few that you will, if ever you use them, soon learn to recognize them. For your convenience, we include here a fraction/decimal conversion table that will be useful for reference.

Common fraction	Decimal fraction
1/2	0.5
1/4	0.25
1/8	0.125
1/3	0.33
1/5	0.2
1/10	0.1

Fractions such as 3/4, 5/8, 4/5 are obtained by simple multiplication. Thus:

$$3/4 = 0.25 \times 3$$
$$= 0.75$$

$$5/8 = 0.125 \times 5$$
$$= 0.625$$

$$4/5 = 0.2 \times 4$$
$$= 0.8$$

Only two sections in this book (4 and 5) call for division by decimal quantities — actually by 7.5 and 4.2, and it is not normally the nurse's responsibility to do them anyway.

The division is very easily done. Six divided by three is two, and six tens or sixty divided by three tens or thirty is also two.

$$\frac{6}{3} = \frac{60}{30}$$

When two numbers are divided into one another they can each be multiplied by the same number without altering the result. So, if you need to divide, for example, 90 by 4.2 you can work in tenths and divide 900 by 42, using long division:

$$
\begin{array}{r}
21.428 \\
\hline
42\,)\,900.0 \\
84 \\
\hline
60 \\
42 \\
\hline
180 \\
168 \\
\hline
120 \\
84 \\
\hline
360 \\
336 \\
\hline
24
\end{array}
$$

so that $90 \div 4.2 = 21.428$

For actual conversion from kJ to Calories these divisions give a result with an entirely spurious appearance of precision. 90 kJ is 20 Calories for all dietetic purposes, and the best way to convert is to use the double scale of Appendix 3.

It does not work out exactly so you continue with decimal division by adding zeros with a decimal separator, as before. There is no need to work it out very far, since the figures you are using (which here give the energy value of a food in two different units) are usually rough anyway. As the text points out on p. 34, it is often good enough to divide by 4 instead of 4.2

A note on calculation

This last section on multiplication and division has been added because the possession of such skills is still expected. This is a reasonable expectation for a profession at the level of nursing, and, occasionally, the skill may be needed. It remains true that the only efficient procedure for anyone who regularly has to do calculations of this kind is the use of a pocket microchip calculator. We hope that nobody is now prepared to argue otherwise.

Try these test questions:

1. 1.25 × 4
2. 0.03 × 5
3. 1.27 × 6
4. 0.001 × 15
5. 14.65 × 3

6. 70 ÷ 4
7. 80 ÷ 4.2
8. 125 ÷ 7.5
9. 15 ÷ 7
10. 2.3 ÷ 5

The answers are on p. 58.

APPENDIX 3

MISCELLANEOUS SCALES AND TABLES

Typical Conversion Scales

A system of measures is only satisfactory if it is used consistently, and SI is designed to cover all ranges of all practical measurement. During a transition period, however, conversion may sometimes be needed to interpret, for example, an unrevised test. The safest and quickest way for general use is a double scale, constructed for the range of values likely to arise.

We give four examples opposite.

The fourth example, of course, needs to be drawn up for each substance under discussion, according to its molecular weight. In the example, glucose has a m.w. of 180.

Answers from p. 57.

1.	5.0	6.	17.5
2.	0.15	7.	16.67
3.	7.62	8.	16.67
4.	0.015	9.	2.14
5.	127.95	10.	0.46

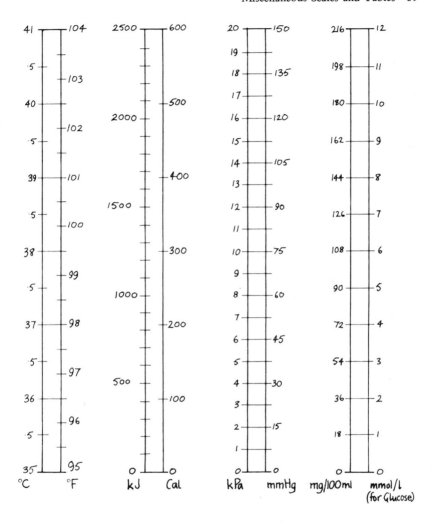

°C	°F	kJ	Cal	kPa	mmHg	mg/100ml	mmol/l (for Glucose)

Age and Weight Tables for Infants

A full account of the relationship between body and weight and age as an indicator of the wellbeing of children is the province of paediatrics. This table is not intended for clinical reference, but merely to give the student nurse the values to be expected when weighing infants. Measuring weight on a modern pointer scale is a straightforward process, but reading unfamiliar graduations is always easier if the results can be anticipated.

Age (months)	Average weight (kg)
0	3.4
1	4.3
2	5.0
3	5.7
6	7.4
12	9.9
18	11.3
24	12.5
30	13.5
36	14.5
48	16.5
60	18.5

Height and Weight Tables for Adults

The height — weight relationship for adults is complex and depends on many factors. This table of values for healthy adults is, like the earlier table, not for clinical reference, but to give the expected values a nurse may find if required to measure these quantities. Because of the wide range of values upper and lower values rather than averages are given.

Men

Height (cm)	Expected weight range (kg)
155	51 — 64
160	54 — 67
165	56 — 71
170	60 — 75
175	60 — 75
180	67 — 84
185	71 — 88
190	74 — 92

Women

Height (cm)	Expected weight range (kg)
145	42 — 53

Height (cm)	Expected weight range (kg)
150	45 — 58
155	48 — 61
160	50 — 64
165	54 — 68
170	57 — 71
175	61 — 76

Energy Values of Foods

It is not the task of nurses to calculate the dietetic value of hospital meals, and it is even less reasonable to expect them to convert from one unit used for this purpose to another. The table below, in SI form, is given to help build up the background of familiarity with measures that a nurse needs to have.

Hospital dieticians, unlike ecologists, rarely need to relate food energy values to those of other sources and tend to stick with the older kilogram – calorie. This table is given in international kilojoules. Nurses might find it interesting as a source of comparison, and note that a sweet biscuit taken during a break provides energy equivalent to six times its own weight of potatoes eaten at lunch! The figures given are rounded average values.

Food	Energy (kJ/100 g)
apples	200
bacon	1 100
butter	3 000
cheese	1 700
cod	350
cod (fried)	950
dates	1 000
eggs	600
olive oil	3 700
potatoes	370
sweet biscuits	2 300
white bread	1 000

Vitamin C in Food

Vitamin C is an essential part of diet because human metabolism is unable to produce it. The list that follows, intended in the first place to give practice in thinking in milligrams, is worth noting when considering a personal diet.

Food	Vitamin C (mg/100g)
brussel sprouts	110
cabbage	70
carrots	8
lettuce	16
oranges	56
pears	4
strawberries	70

A Note on Conversion

Throughout the text of this book we have stressed that the nurse should *never*, as a preliminary to administering drugs or monitoring treatment, be expected to convert from one unit to another by arithmetical calculation.

So many reference books contain conversion factors that a note on their use might be of value to those interested in mathematical details. The problem of conversion is by no means straightforward, as an example will show.

Suppose a child stands on scales (not hospital scales, we hope!) that are calibrated only in stones and pounds, reading to the nearest pound. The weight shown in 4 st. 11 lb. What is this in kilograms? The list in the back of a well known set of tables used in schools gives 0.454 as the conversion factor for pounds to kilograms, so we have 67 lb = 67 × 0.454 kg = 30.418 kg. This does not make sense; we start off with a weight accurate only to the nearest pound and convert it to one accurate apparently to the nearest gram. Not only the value given but the possible error with a more exact measure needs to be converted.

The weight 67 lb could be up to, but not more than, 8 oz out either way if the scales are accurate to the nearest pound. The kilogram equivalent, then, can only be accurate to (roughly) the nearest half kilogram and could be about a quarter kilogram out either way. Even the result 30.4 kg is suspect; it suggests an accuracy of 0.1 kg and a possible error of only 0.05 kg either way. The result should, in fact, be rounded off to the nearest half kilogram and given as 30.5 kg.

A Note on Baby Weight

Nothing in this book will deflect the inevitable follow-up when a nurse in a maternity department answers the queries of expectant relatives, 'What's that in pounds and ounces?'. Here the only solution is a conversion table. Baby weights are usually taken to the nearest 0.01 kg, and the table below converts these to pounds and ounces to the nearest ounce. It must be stressed that the only intended use for this table is to smooth the nurse's contact with the lay public who are not yet accustomed to SI.

kg	0	1	2	3	4	5	6	7	8	9
1.5	3-5	3-5	3-6	3-6	3-6	3-7	3-7	3-7	3-8	3-8
1.6	3-8	3-8	3-9	3-9	3-10	3-10	3-11	3-11	3-11	3-12
1.7	3-12	3-12	3-13	3-13	3-13	3-14	3-14	3-14	3-15	3-15
1.8	3-15	4-0	4-0	4-1	4-1	4-1	4-2	4-2	4-2	4-3
1.9	4-3	4-3	4-4	4-4	4-4	4-5	4-5	4-5	4-6	4-6
2.0	4-7	4-7	4-7	4-8	4-8	4-8	4-9	4-9	4-9	4-10
2.1	4-10	4-10	4-11	4-11	4-11	4-12	4-12	4-12	4-13	4-13
2.2	4-14	4-14	4-14	4-15	4-15	4-15	5-0	5-0	5-0	5-1
2.3	5-1	5-1	5-2	5-2	5-2	5-3	5-3	5-4	5-4	5-4
2.4	5-5	5-5	5-5	5-6	5-6	5-6	5-7	5-7	5-7	5-8
2.5	5-8	5-8	5-9	5-9	5-10	5-10	5-10	5-11	5-11	5-11
2.6	5-12	5-12	5-12	5-13	5-13	5-13	5-14	5-14	5-15	5-15
2.7	5-15	6-0	6-0	6-0	6-1	6-1	6-1	6-2	6-2	6-2
2.8	6-3	6-3	6-3	6-4	6-4	6-4	6-5	6-5	6-6	6-6
2.9	6-6	6-7	6-7	6-7	6-8	6-8	6-8	6-9	6-9	6-9
3.0	6-10	6-10	6-11	6-11	6-11	6-12	6-12	6-12	6-13	6-13

Kilograms to one decimal place are entered in the left hand column, the second decimal place along the top row. The entries are in pounds and ounces separated by a short hyphen.

> Example: 2.67 kg
> Row beginning 2.6, column headed 7
> gives 5 – 14
> 2.67 kg   =   5 lb 14 oz

To convert weights greater than 3 kg divide by 2, look up corresponding value, and then double it.

> Example: 4.42 kg
> Look up 2.21 kg   =   4 lb 14 oz
>   4.42 kg   =   9 lb 12 oz

If the last figure is odd, increase it by 1

> Example: 3.93 kg
> 3.94 kg   =   2 × 1.97 kg
>   =   2 × 4 lb 6 oz
>   =   8 lb 12 oz

Any error introduced by this process is not very different from the rounding errors.

DIAGNOSTIC TEST

1. What is the numerical value of these prefixes?
   - a. milli-
   - b. kilo-
   - c. micro-
   - d. centi-
   - e. deci-
   - f. nano-
2. How many centimetres are in a metre?
3. Make the following conversions:
   - a. 1.6 grams to milligrams
   - b. 0.6 grams to micrograms
   - c. 3.2 litres to millilitres
   - d. 0.3 micrograms to nanograms.
4. Correct the form of the following numerical expressions which are here printed wrongly:
   - a. .35
   - b. 1.273,426
   - c. 1,273
   - d. 2.712,126.
5. Rewrite the number in this prescription correctly: .25 milligrams digoxin.
6. What unit is used in measuring:
   - a. small volumes of liquid (blood samples)?
   - b. large volumes of liquid (petrol)?
7. A 15 mg dose of papaveretum is required from a 20 mg/ml ampoule of solution. How much should be withdrawn?

8. What is the SI unit of pressure?
9. What is the SI unit of temperature?
10. What is the range of a clinical thermometer?
11. In what units is blood pressure usually measured in hospitals?
12. How many millilitres of digoxin elixir (0.05 mg/ml) would you administer to a child requiring 0.20 mg?
13. What is the SI unit of energy?
14. Give the name of a unit often used in hospitals instead of the SI unit of energy.
15. A multidose ampoule contains 75 mg/ml cortisone.
   How many millilitres should be withdrawn for a 50 mg dose?
16. If the molecular weight of common salt (sodium chloride) is 58.5, what is the mass of a mole of salt?
17. Why can you not measure protein in moles?
18. What is the normal body temperature?

If you have only two or three errors or blanks, refer to the relevant pages of the programme. Otherwise you are advised to work through the book at your own speed.

Answers

1. a. 0.001
   b. 1000
   c. 0.000 0001
   d. 0.01
   e. 0.1
   f. 0.000 000 001
2. 100 cm
3. a. 1600 mg
   b. 60 000 g
   c. 3200 ml
   d. 300 ng

4. a. 0.35
   b. 1.273 426
   c. 1273
   d. 2.713 126
5. 0.25 milligram digoxin

6. a. millilitre
   b. litre
7. 0.75 ml
8. the pascal
9. the degree Celsius
10. 35°C – 42°C
11. mmHg
12. 4 ml
13. the joule
14. the calorie*
15. 0.66 ml
16. 58.5 g
17. Because 'protein' is not a substance having a definite molecular weight.
18. 37°C

---

* This is the word commonly used. For the correct form of this word see p. 33.